The Egyptian language changed quite considerably over 4,000 years of use, as did the scripts used to write it down. Alongside the longest lasting, the hieroglyphic script itself, which was basically used for temples, tombs and other important inscriptions, were other forms of writing, used for everyday purposes. *Hieratic* was used in parallel to hieroglyphs and was made up of abbreviated versions of the hieroglyphic signs. *Demotic* was a successor of hieratic, and used to write the developed language of the period from around 700 BC to AD 500, while *Coptic* was a script strongly influenced by Greek letters and was a form of the language used from the third century AD until the Egyptian language was superseded by Arabic during the Middle Ages. But it is the hieroglyphic script that retains the greatest fascination for us because of its nature as a form of picture-writing.

Sacred Writing

To Greek and Roman visitors, like those of today, Egypt was a land of wonders. Its temples, its pyramids and its hieroglyphic picture-writing were quite unlike anything they had seen at home. Like all good tourists they were told tales about what these things meant and the stories behind them. Perhaps the most confusing and most difficult to understand were the hieroglyphics; pyramids as great tombs of despotic kings was an easy concept to grasp, but the carved images of people, animals and inanimate objects – could they really be writing? Surely there are far too many signs here to be an alphabet like that of Greek and Latin? Perhaps they are a special, non-linguistic way of conveying secret information known only to the priests within the temples: the 'Wisdom of the Egyptians'. This is a view which would find favour with a good number of people today. It is, however, wrong.

*S*cene *from the Temple of Amun at Karnak, showing the erection of a pair of inscribed obelisks by King Tuthmosis III.*

MYSTERIES
OF THE ANCIENT WORLD

DECODING
THE STONES

STEVEN SNAPE

WEIDENFELD & NICOLSON

LONDON

T he Egyptian hieroglyphic script is the best known example of a seemingly incomprehensible way of writing invented by ancient peoples, yet one which is understandable to us today. It is, however, only one of several ways of writing used by the Egyptians during their long history.

R ectangular 'serekh' containing one of the names of King Senwosret I, from the White Chapel at Karnak.

It is a misconception that began early in the study of ancient Egypt. The last hieroglyphic inscriptions were written at the end of the 4th century AD (the last dated inscription is AD 394), yet by the second half of the 5th century AD an understanding of the real nature of hieroglyphs had been lost. The author Horapollo Niliacus, seemingly a native Egyptian, wrote his *Hieroglyphica* at this time, in which he described and explained the meaning of hieroglyphic signs. It is clear from this text that at least some knowledge of hieroglyphic writing had survived, since he correctly identifies the meaning of several signs, although often with bizarre explanations of their origins. The vulture, for instance, he correctly identifies as indicating 'mother', yet says this is because 'there is no male of this species of animal'. Other explanations are both bizarre and wrong: 'When they wish to show a man dead from sunstroke they draw a blind beetle, for this dies when blinded by the sun'. Unfortunately the tendency to see Egyptian hieroglyphs not as a way of writing language, but as a higher form of esoteric communication was one which greatly appealed to other Greek and Roman authors, particularly to Pythagorean philosophers, and to European scholars of the Middle Ages and Renaissance, perhaps inspired by publication of Horapollo's work in 1505. The most significant of these European scholars was the German Athanasius Kircher (1602–80), whose valuable work on the Coptic language did not inform his views on hiero-glyphs, which were very much in the tradition of Horapollo in seeing the signs as full of esoteric symbolic meaning. The most famous example of Kircher's 'translations' of hieroglyphic inscriptions being that of the royal name of King Apries, which he read as 'the benefits of the divine Osiris are to be procured by means of sacred ceremonies and of the chain of the Genii, in order that the benefits of the Nile be obtained'.

O **belisk of Queen Hatshepsut at Karnak. In the foreground a block from a Ramesside building.**

*H*ieroglyphs
from the
Pyramid of King
Amenemhat III
at Dahshur.

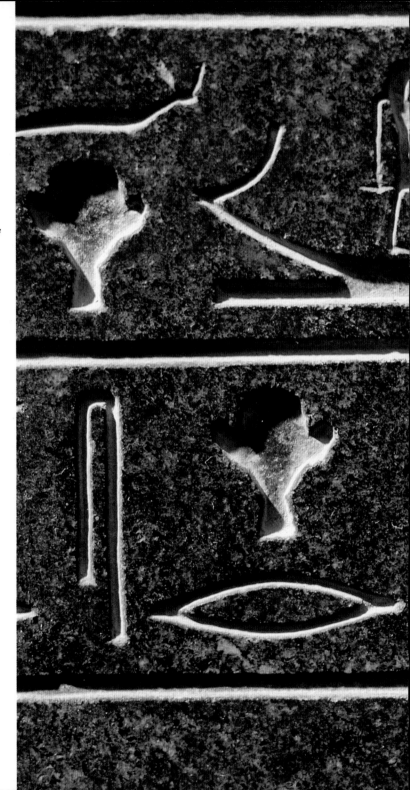

Deciphering Hieroglyphs

The imperial ambitions of Napoleon Bonaparte were to prove instrumental in the decipherment of hieroglyphs. Napoleon's invasion of Egypt in 1799 brought in its wake an army of scholars determined to study this fascinating country. While these savants were labouring in a deliberate search for ancient knowledge, the most significant finding was made by accident. The Rosetta Stone was found while digging the foundations for a fort near the coastal city of Rashid. The stone bears a temple decree dating to the reign of King Ptolemy V: 27 March 196 BC. Its importance is that the same text is inscribed three times on the stone: once in Egyptian hieroglyphs, with copies in Greek and demotic. The texts on the stone became the objects of determined study because the translated Greek text could act as a guide to the translation of the hieroglyphic version.

The royal names on the stone were the most obvious way into the text. It had already been correctly guessed that the groups of signs contained by the oval surround called a cartouche were in fact royal names. The English scholar Thomas Young (1773–1829) was able to identify the cartouche that corresponded to the name Ptolemy in the Greek text and work out phonetic values for the hieroglyphic signs. However, Young decided that phonetic signs were only used to write non-Egyptian names and that most hieroglyphs were of a symbolic nature. It was left to the French scholar Jean-François Champollion (1790–1832) to achieve fame as the cracker of the hieroglyphic code. Champollion began by using the now-known values of the name Ptolemy and then went on to use another bilingual Greek and Egyptian

The Rosetta Stone proved to be the key to the understanding of hieroglyphs.

text, the Bankes obelisk, to apply these known signs to the name Cleopatra and therefore work out the values of those signs in her name that do not appear in Ptolemy. From here it was a logical step to translate other royal names and then other words, using the Coptic language as a guide to the meaning of the decoded words.

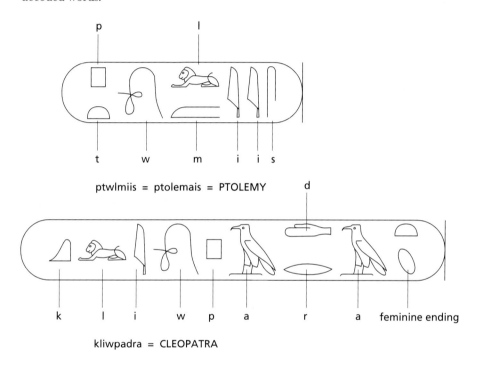

ptwlmiis = ptolemais = PTOLEMY

kliwpadra = CLEOPATRA

The publication of Champollion's discoveries in 1824 marked the beginning of scholarship which was to gradually reveal the true nature of the hieroglyphic script and the language it was used to write, so that the inscriptions of the Egyptians and what they really contained could be revealed after a 'dark age' of 1,500 years.

Cleopatra's Needle in Alexandria, from a watercolour of 1813.

Khufu/Cheops (2251–2228 BC):
builder of the great pyramid at Giza

*R*oyal names: some
of the best-known
Egyptian kings.

Amenemhat: name of four kings
of the 12th Dynasty (1991–1783 BC)

Senwosret I (1971–1926 BC):
king of the 12th Dynasty

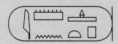

Amenhotep: name of four kings
of the 18th Dynasty (1550–1307 BC)

Tuthmosis: name of four kings
of the 18th Dynasty (1150–1307 BC)

Hatshepsut (1473–1458 BC): regent for Tuthmosis III
and ruling queen of the 18th Dynasty

Tuthmosis III (1479–1425 BC):
warrior-king of the 18th Dynasty

Amenhotep III (1391–1353 BC):
king when Egypt's empire was at its height

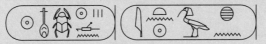

Akhenaten (1353–1335 BC):
royal religious reformer of the 'Amarna Period'

Tutankhamen (1333–1323 BC)

Ramesses II (1290–1224 BC)

Psammetichus I (664–610 BC): king of the 26th Dynasty

Nectanebo: name of two kings of the 30th Dynasty
(380–343 BC), the last native-born Egyptian Dynasty

Alexander the Great (356–323 BC)

The Use of Hieroglyphs

There is a very obvious difference between Egyptian hieroglyphs and most other scripts ancient and modern – its forms are derived from the real world and are not simply a set of distinctive, but individually meaningless squiggles like our alphabet. Staring at this page, or at the wedge-impressed surface of a cuneiform tablet, someone unfamiliar with both (say, a member of a lost tribe in the Amazon Basin) would, understandably, stare blankly at both page and tablet. However, a wall covered with Egyptian hieroglyphs would contain a whole range of familiar images; a fish, a bird, parts of the human body. The question might reasonably be asked, does this sign which looks like a bird represent something to do with a bird? The answer is sometimes yes, sometimes no. The whole nature of hieroglyphic writing is neither so simple as an obvious equation of image and real object, nor as difficult as the bizarre explanations of the Horapollo/Kircher school, but is part of a consistent and rational system of writing.

Although it may appear complex and exclusive, the purpose of hieroglyphic script was to communicate, albeit to a rather restricted audience of the Egyptian literate elite and, of course, the gods themselves. It was a form of writing developed for use in places where the beauty of the script itself was important and each sign could be lovingly crafted. This is in contrast to its cursive counterpart, hieratic, which was designed to be written quickly with a minimum number of penstrokes. Hieroglyphic was predominantly the script of the stonecarver and painter and its name (from the Greek *hieros*: 'sacred'; and *glypho*: 'sculpted') suggests that it was indeed used for texts that carried

Tomb painting from the mastaba tomb of Rahotep and Nofret.

E xquisitely carved hieroglyphs from the White Chapel of Senwosret I, giving the name of the chapel.

V ulture hieroglyph from the temple of Amun at Karnak.

important eternal truths and used in temples (houses of the gods, built for eternity) and tombs (houses of the dead, built for eternity); the stone wall of the infinite temple carrying the infinite text. The Egyptians themselves called the hieroglyphic script *mdw nṯr* 'the god's words', and most hieroglyphic texts were records of royal activities, texts from sacred writings, lists of rituals to be performed, and wishes for the afterlife. Hieroglyphic script is used where the human world meets the divine and a permanent and distinctive expression is required to mark the event.

Hieroglyphs were therefore a very traditional form of writing and generally resistant to change, although new words do appear from time to time – inscriptions relating royal victories over foreign enemies of the New Kingdom would be hard put to dispense with the new word 'chariot'. The language of hieroglyphs was that which we call Middle Egyptian, and even when spoken Egyptian itself changed with time, hieroglyphs tended to be slow in absorbing these changes. The anachronistic nature of the language may itself have been a positive element, giving an authority to the message of the text, in the same way that the English of the King James Bible may carry extra authority for a 20th-century reader. The script may also have had a timeless quality for the Egyptians in the same way that Latin dedicatory inscriptions were placed on the public buildings of the 19th century.

The hieroglyphic caption above this figure gives him the title 'royal scribe', while the cobra later added to his brow identifies his ascendancy to the throne as King Horemheb.

Hieroglyph of a striding lion carved in granite (overleaf); from the temple of Amun at Tanis.

Types of Sign

The earliest type of hieroglyphic signs are the pictorial
labels attached to objects in the late Predynastic period
(before 3100 BC). This is a type of 'writing' that is very
easy for anyone to understand; a simple representation
of, for example, a loaf of bread or a jug of beer, followed
by the appropriate number of vertical strokes can repre-
sent 0 ||| '5 loaves of bread' or ||||| '8 jars of beer'.
By the beginning of the First Dynasty (3100 BC) the
need to develop a way of representing spoken language
in a written form resulted in a number of developments
in the evolution of the hieroglyphic script. Two types of
sign developed. The first of these was the logogram
where an object was represented by a hieroglyphic sign
that looked like the object itself, such as 'bull'.
This is clear and straightforward, but very limiting when
it comes to writing more complex sentences. For
instance, on the slate palette representing King Narmer
and a fallen enemy, the group of signs to the right of
the king *might* be regarded as a label to the scene, read-
ing, 'The falcon-god Horus overcomes the people of
the marsh-land', or it may be a picture of that event

happening – the boundary between illustration and writing is very blurred.

More complex ideas and more complex sentences would pose even greater
problems. For this reason most hieroglyphic signs do not stand for the thing
they look like but are employed for their phonetic value. For instance, we have
already seen that Horapollo correctly identified the sign for a vulture as stand-
ing for 'mother'. The correct explanation for why this should be is the rebus

*B*rightly painted figures and hieroglyphic texts of deities of inundation and plenty from the Abydos Temple of King Ramesses II.

principle, whereby things can be represented not by signs that look like the object, but by signs representing objects that have a similar sound. The Egyptian word for vulture was pronounced 'mwt', but the word for mother was also pronounced 'mwt'. In this way a whole range of words that were not easy to

A **papyrus copy**
of the religious
text, the Book of the
Dead.

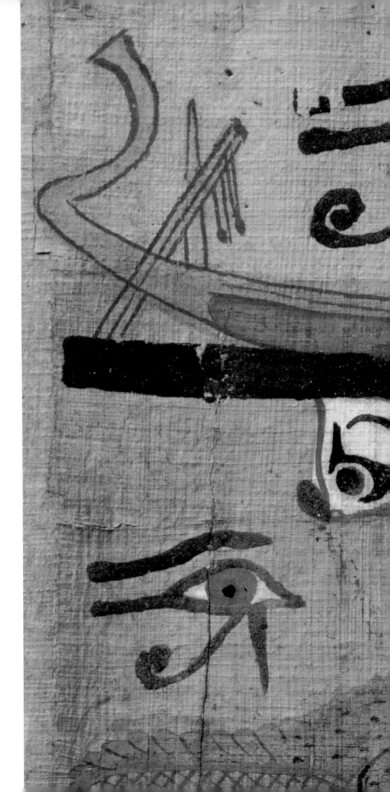

represent by single pictorial signs could be rendered by signs that were pronounced the same. This idea is already present on the Narmer palette, the name of the king himself being written with two signs, *Nar* (the nar-fish) and *Mr* (the word for chisel).

An extension of this idea was to have a range of particularly common signs that were used for their phonetic value which in English we render by one letter ($\vert$ = *s*), or two letters ($\square$ = *pr*) or, less commonly, three letters ($\frac{1}{\delta}$ = *nfr*). These signs are called phonograms. But phonograms and logograms are often used together in a single word, where the phonograms spell out how a word is to be pronounced, while a logogram at the end of the word acts as a determinative, making clear the meaning of a word. For example, in the verb ⟨hieroglyphs⟩ *wbn*, 'to shine', the signs ⟨sign⟩ = *w*, ⟨sign⟩ = *b*, ⟨sign⟩ = *n* and the sign ⟨sign⟩ shows what the word is about. This is useful for words which sound the same but have different meanings such as the word *sr* written with the simple signs for s and r but which , according to the determinative used can mean a type of goose (⟨goose sign⟩), a ram (⟨ram sign⟩), and official (⟨official sign⟩), or the verb 'to foretell' (⟨giraffe sign⟩ the appropriate determinative of a far-seeing giraffe!).

*T*he so-called White Chapel of King Senwosret I
from the Karnak Temple, Thebes, famous for its
finely carved limestone reliefs and hieroglyphs.

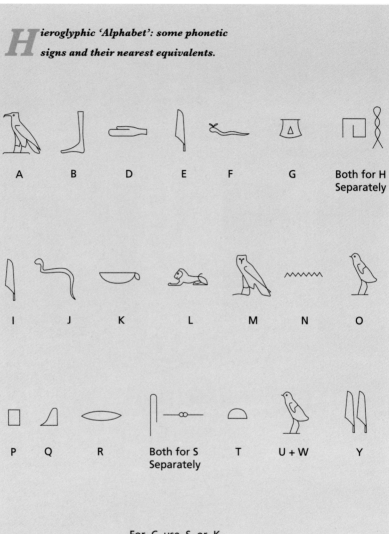

*H*ieroglyphic 'Alphabet': some phonetic
signs and their nearest equivalents.

A   B   D   E   F   G   Both for H
Separately

I   J   K   L   M   N   O

P   Q   R   Both for S   T   U + W   Y
Separately

For C use S or K

For V use F

For X use K + S

For Z use S

| = 1   ∩ = 10

◠ = 100   = 1,000

= 10,000   = 100,000

= 1,000,000

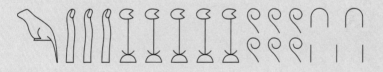

100,000	x 1
10,000	x 3
1,000	x 5
100	x 6
10	x 2
1	x 3

= 135,623

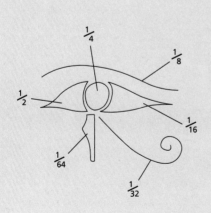

H **ieroglyphic numbers.**
Fractions could be
formed by using parts of
the eye of the god Horus.

One of the benefits of the hieroglyphic system is that the text can be written from left to right or right to left in horizontal lines, or top to bottom in vertical columns. This makes it particularly suitable for inscribing individual parts of temple and tomb buildings; not just walls but columns, pillars and around doorways, where parallel inscriptions on each side of the doorway are often direct mirror-images of each other. The direction in which the script is read is, as a rule, the direction in which the signs of the text face, but a major consideration in the arrangement of the text on the wall was its appearance, and the ability to choose one of several signs for common phonetic values facilitated a pleasing grouping of signs without unsightly gaps.

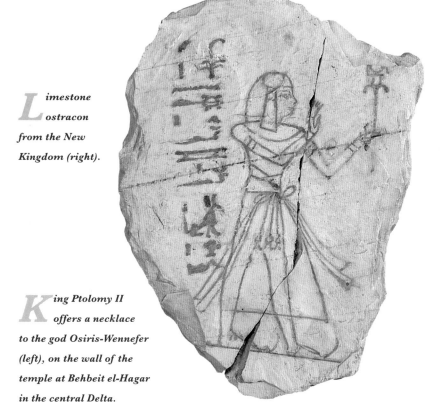

*L*imestone *ostracon from the New Kingdom (right).*

*K*ing Ptolomy II *offers a necklace to the god Osiris-Wennefer (left), on the wall of the temple at Behbeit el-Hagar in the central Delta.*

A bydos kinglist:
Prince Ramesses
assists his father, Seti I,
in offering to the names of
their royal predecessors.

By the Ptolemaic period (332–30 BC) hieroglyphic script had become detached from the normal spoken and written language of everyday Egyptians. The cursive script, demotic, was the way in which contemporary Egyptian language was written, a language that had altered considerably since the period of the Middle Kingdom, some 2,000 years before. Therefore both the hieroglyphic script and the Middle Egyptian stage of the language which it was